The Things In Your Head

written by Kimberly Johnson

illustrated by Jill E. Buffington

BuLu™ is a trademark of Inspired Girl Productions
www.theadventuresofbulu.com

ISBN-13: 978-0615680507
ISBN-10: 061568050X

DEDICATION

To Lucas & Madison, my AMAZING gifts. You both have taught me so much about being your Mom. I adore you both and I am so grateful you chose me to be your Mom.

ACKNOWLEDGEMENTS

To my Dad; without you, I would not be the person I am, thank you & I miss you every single day.
To my Mom; who gave me my love of books, thank you.
To my dear friend Colette Baron-Reid, for EVERYTHING, I adore you & thank you.
To my friend Lisa Toste-Karayan, who gave me the shove to finish this book, encouraged me all along the way, thank you.
To my partner in creativity, Jill. Thank you for believing in this and making it STUNNING.
And to my partner, Mark, for putting up with our crazy life and loving me anyway.

DEDICATION

To my Grandma Buffington who gave me the artistic tools and inspiration to be creative at a very young age, and for her constant support, constructive criticism, and encouragement in all of my works.

ACKNOWLEDGEMENTS

Thank you to my Mom and Dad who have showered me with love, patience, and understanding all of my life. I have greatly appreciated how you both have fostered my creative energies as a child, and am thankful for your continual support of my projects into my adulthood.

PARENT'S GUIDE

When I was a child I worried about everything. I worried about missing the bus. I worried about not having my homework done. Mostly common kid worries, however, one summer I became very concerned that my father would die. I remember wondering over and over and over again how to stop the thoughts, really to no avail. If I were a child in today's world, I probably would have been diagnosed OCD. But in the 70s that was not the case. My strategy to stop worrying was to flood my head by reading. I would devour science-fiction books, going to a place of fantasy to keep my mind busy. I would draw, paint, or read most of my free time. As an only child I learned to be very self-sufficient with keeping myself occupied although keeping my mind occupied in the background was always a challenge.

Fast forward to the 1990s, I discovered Anthony Robbins. I began reading his books, listening to his tapes and eventually attending his seminars. I finally had found strategies, ways to control my emotions, my thoughts and realized that this is not a curse, this is a gift.

I made the decision to dedicate myself to understanding human emotions and went to work for Anthony Robbins. For the next 10 years my life I was consumed with learning and understanding as much as I could about people, their emotions, and how they end up where they are emotionally.
During this time I was raising my daughter as a single mom having gone through a divorce that was not pretty. Her mindset became my priority. The way she saw the world and the situation we were in was so important to me. In order for her to feel good about herself, I had to make sure the thoughts that I was putting into her head were not toxic, but filled with love.

I made mistakes, I cried, and I loved her more than anything in my life. She was my motivation at that time to become better at who I was as a person, as well as a mom.

Every live event for Anthony Robbins I would attend, I would meet more and more people who had challenges with their belief system. And over the course of time I came to believe that the missing piece of the puzzle was teaching children when they are very small how to control their thoughts and feelings. What would happen if you instilled a strong belief systems about thoughts, feelings and emotions in a toddler? What would happen to that child if they never had the negative thoughts enter their mind? Or better yet, if they did enter, there was zero attachment or reaction.

Empowering children should be our most important goal. Filling their minds and their hearts with so much love and certainty about their own identities that no one else can put in any poison. So when the bully shows up or the person who makes a comment that they're stupid or not enough, it has little or no effect. The child immediately understands this is an unhappy person who's speaking to them.

The child has a developed skill set that allows them to discern that the comments and actions mean absolutely nothing to them. With the right emotional building blocks, the child can even understand compassion for the person, knowing that there is something sad within them that causes this behavior.

Teaching children this from the earliest age is imperative. Kindness and compassion with their own pets, siblings and parents. Your home is the earliest classroom and from the time the child is born, he is learning. You are a teacher whether you like it or not. You are the first and strongest example for them. Modeling behavior is something that Mother Nature provides to all mammals, including humans.

The first lesson is this; love yourself and then your child can love themselves.
Put forth in your own behavior what you would like to see in them. All too often we are consumed with business, life, and stress, rushing around, void of compassion and kindness for others, not to mention ourselves!

This book is designed to begin the process of recognizing negative thoughts and changing them to positive thoughts as soon as they arrive. As BuLu goes from sad to happy, your child will learn the building blocks of Nero Linguistic Programming and change his physical state of being as well as the thoughts in his head.

It is meant to be fun and active! Read the story with your child and act it out with him. You will be surprised just how quickly and well it works.
And most importantly, help yourself by managing your own thoughts. This process, while it may seem silly, works just as well for adults as it does for children.

I wish you and your child a lifetime of happy, healthy thoughts & words.
Thank you for following BuLu on this adventure and the many others he is about to embark on!

Smile always,
Kim

Have you ever considered the THINGS in your head...

The things that you THINK as you lie there in bed?

Thoughts float in and thoughts float out...

Your mind is the place where IDEAS can sprout!

This is the place where you BECOME you...

And what you BELIEVE really can come true!

Words will DESCRIBE **the thoughts in your mind...**

It's here to be CAREFUL and see what you find.

Can't...don't...and won't are the WORDS of worst case,

It's their job to wipe the SMILE off your face.

So when they pop in, just scream "STOP!!!"

"I'm not meant for the bottom, I will be on TOP"

Put your fingers in your EARS and turn roundabout,

It's time to act crazy and a little WACKED out!

Stand on one foot and DO the bunny hop...

Jump up in the air and DANCE the bee bop!

The thoughts you create should be a HAPPY focus,

This is the magic, the REAL *Hocus Pocus*!

I CAN, I WILL, I MUST are the words that do just fine,

They are words that make sure you SHINE!

Use the fun words, the ones that are RARE...

Even make up your own to show that you CARE!

Feed your mind HEALTHY words throughout the day,

They will keep you INSPIRED and well on your way!

Made in the USA
Middletown, DE
27 January 2021